ENVIRONMENT

Re-use t
Carrier bag

RUTH VALERIO

Published 2008 by CWR, Waverley Abbey House, Waverley Lane, Farnham, Surrey GU9 8EP, UK. Registered Charity No. 294387. Registered Limited Company No. 1990308.

See back of book for list of National Distributors.

Unless otherwise indicated, all Scripture references are from the Holy Bible: New International Version (NIV), copyright © 1973, 1978, 1984 by the International Bible Society.

Other Bible version used:
The Message, copyright © 1993, 1994, 1995, 1996, 2000, 2001, 2002. Used by permission of NavPress Publishing Group.

Concept development, editing, design and production by CWR.

Printed in England by Nuffield Press
Nuffield Press is an ISO14001, FSC and PEFC registered printer. The lamination and adhesive used on the cover are sustainable, compostable and can be recycled. The paper used in this book is made of up to 100% recycled fibre or paper.

ISBN: 978-1-85345-481-3

CONTENTS

INTRODUCTION

I once made a William Morris tapestry of a peacock. Intricate and very beautiful, it took a lot of work to complete. Now, it hangs proudly on our sitting room wall. I wonder how I would feel if I found my children using it as a doormat to wipe their muddy feet on? I wonder how God feels with the way we are treating His intricate and beautiful world, as we tread on it and make it filthy?

The morning I began writing this *Life Issues* study guide, I was stopped in the playground by a mum wanting to ask me about the chickens we keep in our back garden. She said, 'Do you know, Ruth, you fascinate me. I've got to ask you, why do you do the things you do and live the way you do?' The only answer I could give was that it was because of my Christian faith; that I wanted to live in a way that respected the world God had made and that I saw the way I lived as part of how I worshipped Him. Did that sound bizarre, I asked my friend? No, she said, she thought it was great.

Another day, I dropped my children off to play at their friend's house. As I walked in, their dad started firing questions at me. He had been watching a television programme that included a debate between a 'greenie' talking about the changes we should make in our lives, and a professor who dismissed it, saying that there is no use doing anything because of India and China. My friend's husband thought the professor had a point and wanted to know what my opinion was. We ended up in a discussion that lasted most of the afternoon!

These three illustrations take us to the heart of this study guide. Our world is facing immense problems that we cannot ignore, and people are concerned. By and large, people's world-views are shaped by what they watch on the television and read in the newspapers, and this only serves to make them more confused and, very often, feeling hopeless.

And what about us? What do these problems have to do with our Christian faith? Peter told his listeners always to 'be prepared to give an answer to everyone who asks you to give the reason for the hope that you have' (1 Pet. 3:15). Is this relevant to ecological concerns? What hope can we offer our seemingly hopeless world? Does it matter anyway if the world is spoilt – after all, don't science and the Bible both say that it is going to be destroyed in the end? What does the Bible say about this fragile earth, and how we should view it?

In this study guide, we will be making our way through this maze of questions. In order to do this, each week will be divided into three main sections:

The first section will follow the biblical story. So, we will begin with the story of creation and all that teaches us about God, our world and our place within it. Next, we will look at the Fall and at what went wrong. In Week Three we will look more generally at the Old Testament and the place of the land within the nation of Israel. Finally, we will look at our future hope.

The second section will look at particular issues that are facing our world and its inhabitants today. Thus, through our four weeks together we will consider climate change, deforestation, species extinction and water problems.

The third section will focus on things we can all do to respond practically to the world, in the light of the biblical teaching. So, we will look at the food we eat, the way we travel, the energy we use, and the things we throw away.

Author's Note:
Much of the material from the Issues and Responses sections have been adapted from R. Valerio, *L is for Lifestyle: Christian Living that Doesn't Cost the Earth* (Leicester: IVP, 2008), and statistical references can be found there. You will also notice, as you read through, that the Responses sections do not follow on from the Issues. This is quite deliberate, as due to the complexity of the subject, the issues raised and our general response feed into each other, flowing together as a whole.

SOME FURTHER POINTS FOR GROUPS:
- *Discussion groups always work best when people have read the material through beforehand. So ask your group to do that.*
- *This book contains space within the material for your own thoughts and notes. Please encourage people to have a pen/pencil ready to jot down any comments or questions, both when they read the material beforehand and also whilst discussing it.*
- *You might consider ending each week by asking people to commit to one practical change they will make to their lives, and then start the following session by informally sharing what has happened, before the study begins.*

May you be stretched, challenged and inspired!

THE WONDER OF CREATION

◎ To open with

Share together your most vivid memories of nature from childhood. What were the sights, the sounds, the smells that stuck in your mind?

◎ Read

Genesis 1 and 2

◎ Thinking together

For many years, the main purpose of these familiar chapters has been for use as a weapon in the arguments around evolution, science and the Bible. But we miss the point when we focus solely on those debates. When these creation narratives were written, Israel's neighbouring nations had their own stories about how they believed the world came into existence, which informed their understanding of their gods and the meaning of the world and people. Much of what we have in the Genesis accounts acts as a polemic against the implicit theology that came out from those creation stories and they are crucial to our understanding of God, our world and of our place within that world. Let us highlight four things.

Firstly, Christians believe that the God who made the world is a trinity: God is an *us* not a *me*. In a seminar, I once asked why God made the world, and someone answered, 'Because He was lonely.' Well, I understand the sentiment behind that, but theologically that is not really the case. It is important to understand that God did not make the world because He was in need of it, because that implies that God lacks something. God was already a full and complete community of relations in the Trinity.

No, God made the world simply for its own sake. This means that the world has *intrinsic* value: value in-and-of-itself. It does not exist for our sake. Its value does not lie in what it can do for us. Its ultimate value lies in its creation by a loving God who had no inherent need for it, but simply a desire that it exist.

Secondly, when God looked at all that He had made, both human and non-human, He saw that it was 'very good' (1:31). These two little words, 'very good', mean that God thought this world amazing. Our Christian tradition, tangled up with Greek philosophical ideas, has sometimes taught us to make a distinction between tangible, earthly stuff (what we have called 'physical') and intangible, heavenly stuff (what we have called 'spiritual'). However, not only is this a false distinction, but the tangible, earthly stuff is very important to God. Matter matters to God!

Thirdly, creation is never considered to be a finished work: rather, it is a dynamic process; a project to be completed. Some scholars have noticed that the usual refrain, 'And there was evening, and there was morning – the first [second, third etc] day', is missing from the end of the seventh day. Why? Could it be because 'God's work of unfolding and developing the inbuilt potential of creation throughout human history'[1] is continuing? To put this in theological terms, creation has a *telos*, a goal, and Colossians 1:16 explains this more – creation exists for the sake of Christ.

Fourthly, we see the place of humanity in God's creation. On the one hand we must never forget that we are a part of creation; formed from the earth on the same day as other animals; living within the same ecosystems and sharing the same food (Gen. 1:29–30). And yet, alone of all that God created, humans are made 'in the image of God' (Gen. 1:27 – see also v.26). The Hebrew grammar of this verse carries the sense of 'Let us make humanity in our own image, in our likeness, *so that* they may rule over …' It is almost as if God had in His mind (so to speak!) that He would create humankind *in order that* they might look after the rest of His creation.[2] The idea here comes from the nations around Israel in which the king was thought to be the representative of the gods and, in this sense, was described as the gods' 'image', representing the presence of the gods in the midst of the people. We, therefore, as the image of God, are to be God's representatives on earth; placed here to 'take care' (Gen. 2:15) of the rest of creation and enable it to fulfil its purpose of existing for God's glory. If we flagrantly spoil or ruin God's creation, we are not being good stewards of His gift.

For discussion

- *Have you ever considered before just* why *God made the world?*
- *Which areas of Church life do you think have been especially affected by the distinction between the 'spiritual' and 'physical' view?*
- *'... creation is never considered to be a finished work ... [but] a project to be completed.' How does this challenge existing ideas about science, medicine, agriculture etc?*
- *If a part of our reason for existence is to look after the rest of what God has made, how should we respond spiritually – and practically?*

The issue: Climate change

'Oh, it's probably due to climate change,' said my window cleaner as we chatted about the weather. Some say we are getting paranoid about climate change, but others argue that this is with good reason, because climate change is now recognised as being the biggest threat facing us and our planet today.

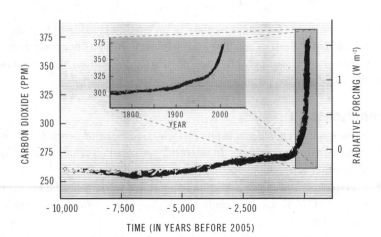

This graph shows the amount of carbon dioxide (CO_2) that has been in the atmosphere in the 10,000 years prior to 2005 and the massive increase that has taken place in the years since the Industrial Revolution.[3] As is well documented, CO_2 is one of a host of 'greenhouse gases' that trap the sun's heat in the atmosphere, leading to global warming, which results in the climate changing. The Intergovernmental Panel on Climate Change (the scientific global authority) made this statement in 2007:

Warming of the climate system is unequivocal, as is now evident from observations of increases in global average air and ocean temperatures, widespread melting of snow and ice, and rising global average sea level. Most of the observed increase in global average temperatures since the mid-20th century is very likely (>90%) due to the observed increase in anthropogenic greenhouse gas concentrations.

The consequences are hard to predict, both because they are partly dependent on our response now (if we significantly reduce our CO_2 emissions the consequences will be different to if we do very little to respond), and also because there are unforeseen variables that can feed back into the process, speeding up climate change beyond the predictions (for example, it was discovered that as snow/ice melts, the reflective white cover on the ground is replaced by black rock or soil that absorbs the heat, thus increasing global warming).

Even were we to stop all emissions tomorrow, however, we *do* know that we are already set on a path of global warming, the consequences of which are horrendous. It is likely that the Greenland icecap will melt, eventually leading to a 7m sea rise. An initial rise of only 1m will affect 100 million people globally. There will be more intense heatwaves, floods and droughts. Millions of species will be lost globally and there will be an estimated 150 million environmental refugees by 2050. As is so often the case, it is the poorest nations and people who will be the worst affected.

◎ The response: The food we eat

Food is the area in which we have the biggest environmental impact. Five issues in particular stand out here. The first is our high levels of meat/dairy consumption. A report by the UN's Food and Agricultural Organization has stated that the livestock industry is 'one of the top two or three most significant contributors to the most serious environmental problems, at every scale from local to global', contributing to land degradation, climate change, air pollution, water shortage and water pollution, and loss of biodiversity.[4]

Secondly, the government's recommendation to wash or peel fruit and vegetables before eating highlights the routine use of many chemicals to grow the produce we eat and the potential dangers to our health that they pose, not to mention the damage done to the land. A Cox apple can receive thirty-six different pesticides through sixteen separate sprayings!

Thirdly is the issue of 'food miles'. This is not simple as it is often the case that a product grown in and transported from a less economically developed country has less overall food miles than one grown in and transported from a wealthier country. Nonetheless, in general we should aim for our food to have travelled as short a distance as possible to reach our plates.

Fourthly, Proverbs 12:10 says that the righteous care for the needs of their animals and the issue of how our meat is reared and produced is very important. Should we as Christians accept intensive farming practices and buy the products (particularly chicken, eggs, prawns, salmon and pork) that come from them?

Finally is the issue of power. The biotechnology companies producing the pesticides; the big food manufacturers influencing what kind of food is grown and the supermarkets controlling distribution and dictating prices and uniformity of produce, all mean that power is taken out of the hands of those who produce the food and those who consume it.

WHAT CAN I DO?

- *Consider swapping a meat-based meal for a meat-less one each week.*
- *If possible, subscribe to an organic veg box delivery (see the Organic Directory at www.whyorganic.org).*
- *Grow some of your own food this year (even just a few herbs in a pot, if you are short of space). Do you have a local Farmers' Market or farm shop you could use?*
- *Try to buy meat, fish and seafood that is free range, organic, or 'freedom food' (MSC for fish/sea food) certified.*
- *If there is a Fairtrade alternative, buy it!*

◎ Engaging with God

'God saw all that he had made, and it was very good' (Gen. 1:31). Use this as a basis of worship as you reflect on this session. Thank God for His creation, for the beauty seen in your childhood, and today. Praise Him for His faithfulness. If there is time, sing a worship song or hymn that glorifies God as Creator.

THE TRAGEDY OF THE FALL

◎ To open with

Let each person write down three things, in order of importance, that worry them most about the world as it is today. Compare lists, and spend some time talking about why each item is of such great concern.

◎ Read

Genesis 3

◎ Thinking together

God made a world that reflected who He is, and so His creation has relationships built into the very fabric of its being. Those relationships exist on all levels: we only have to consider how we are all part of one massive ecosystem, and also lots of smaller inter-related webs, to see that this is the case. Classically in theology these relationships exist between God, human beings and the rest of creation. It can be drawn diagrammatically like this:

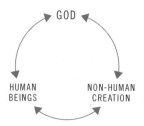

So, when God made the world, He did so with the desire that there would be good relationships flowing in all directions: between God and us, between God and the non-human creation, between us and the rest of creation, and between ourselves. It could also be argued that there were to be good relationships within the non-human creation as well, with no carnivores, but that is a subject for debate!

The tragedy, however, is that everything soon went badly wrong. It is interesting to look at the story of the Fall and its effects through the grid of these relationships; as we do so, we see how each relationship became damaged as a result.

In Genesis 3:8 we glimpse how our relationship with God was originally intended to be. All of us who have been to a hot country know how special the 'cool of the day' is (*The Message* translates this phrase as 'the evening breeze'): a time to relax after the heat and work of the day and enjoy one another's company. Although we already know that things have gone wrong, the picture of God walking in the cool of the evening, in and with His creation, is beautiful. But Adam and Eve hide from God. The naturalness and ease has gone. They are now scared of God; the relationship has been broken.

The first impact we see of Adam and Eve's sin is the effect it has on the non-human creation. The snake in Genesis 3 is literally a snake and there will now be 'enmity' between the snake and the woman. Later interpretation has read this as being the 'proto-evangelium', a first indication of the gospel message; Satan has exploited the human decision to rebel. However, as we read Genesis 3 without reference to the New Testament teaching, we can see that it clearly shows human rebellion has set us at odds with God and His creation – as well as with each other.

More strikingly, in 3:17, God tells Adam that the ground is now cursed because of him. Note the Hebrew wordplay: the *adamah* ('ground') is cursed because of *adam* (literally, 'earthling' or 'earth creature'). Now, it will be hard to produce food from the land: again that naturalness and easiness has gone. The close link between ourselves and the ground from which we have come is broken.

Finally, in the words that God speaks to Eve (3:16) we see the effects of the Fall on our relationships with one another. The word for 'desire' is the same as that used in 4:7 where God warns Cain that sin is crouching at his door and desires to have him. This is not about romantic love, but about a desire for domination and control. Despite the woman's intention to control the man, though, the man instead will rule over the woman. Thus we see the start of the battle of the sexes and, in general, of disharmony between people.

In verse 21, we are told that 'The LORD God made garments of skin for Adam and his wife and clothed them'. In the midst of His punishment and our relational disasters, God works an act of grace. This happens constantly throughout the biblical narrative: in God giving Cain his 'mark' (4:15); in God choosing Noah and his family and the other creatures to survive the Flood; in God choosing Abram and Sarai after the debacle of Babel and, ultimately, in the gift of Jesus. Thus, whilst this week seems depressing, we know that hope is coming.

For discussion

- *As you think back to Genesis 1 and 2, where do you see harmony in relationships, as God designed them to be?*
- *Consider some of the items that have been in the news this week. How do they reflect the fact that relationships between God, humans and the non-human creation are damaged?*
- *Do you feel connected with God, other people, and the rest of creation? Are there any areas where you feel disconnected?*
- *We have looked at God's 'acts of grace' in a broken world. Have you personally seen or experienced such acts?*

◎ The issue: Deforestation

What can you see around you that has been made from wood? Shockingly, the UK is the fifth highest consumer of paper in the world, despite its tiny size. Now let us think through our eating habits. How often do we eat beef, particularly from fast food outlets? Can we guarantee that it was not reared in South/Latin America on rainforest land? How many of the products we buy from the supermarket (to eat and use) contain vegetable oil? Are we aware that this may be palm oil, grown on vast plantations in Malaysia and Indonesia that used to be rainforest? It is thought that if these plantations continue, the orang-utan could be extinct by 2017. Have we ever thought about where our aluminium foil comes from? Or our tin cans? Have we ever asked our banks whether our money is used to finance projects that are cutting down forests? What about biofuels that are heralded as a green solution to petrol: on what land are they primarily grown?

What a horrific list of questions to bombard us with! But we are inextricably connected to the world's forests and we forget that connection at our peril. At its most basic we need the forests because they absorb CO_2 and emit oxygen. Thus deforestation is the second main source of climate change, behind burning fossil fuels. We also need the rainforest for our medicine and food. Rainforest plants have contributed to 25 per cent of the medicine we use today and yet over 99 per cent of tropical plants are still to be tested for their chemical compounds. Similarly, an amazing amount of our food has come from the rainforest and we need the genetic material from the wild strains in order to maintain the strength and health of the modern stock.

But we have forgotten our connectedness. There is now no original forest left in India, Bangladesh, Sri Lanka and Haiti. Over two million hectares of rainforest have been cut down in Indonesia, mainly due to the demand for palm oil. Millions of people globally live in and/or depend on forests for their livelihood and it is thought that an acre of rainforest land is six times more financially lucrative if sustainably harvested than if cut down for commercial use. Once cut down, of course, the land quickly loses its fertility, leading to flooding and soil erosion and an inability to support either agriculture or cattle.

◎ The response: The way we travel

Last week we saw the huge issue of climate change and its staggering implications for our world. As is well known, our driving and flying habits contribute significantly as we use increasing amounts of petrol and diesel to get ourselves around.

Road traffic is the fastest growing source of air pollution and yet, despite what we know about the damaging effects of cars, nearly 29 million new ones are made each year and car traffic is expected to increase by 22 per cent by 2010. One of the biggest problems is not only that increasing numbers of people are buying cars, but that we are using them more often and for shorter journeys. In the UK 25 per cent of car trips are less than two miles and just under two-thirds are less than five miles.

Hybrid cars are slowly increasing in popularity, electric cars are available for short distances and biofuels are being looked into, but none of these are the ultimate answer. What would a world look like in which we all drove cars, even if they were 'clean'? The reality is that cars not only consume energy (even 'clean' cars have to be made out of something) but they lead to massive road building, prevent us keeping fit by cycling or walking, divorce us from the world around us (can you hear the birds sing or see/smell the flowers in a car?) and increase our culture of individualisation.

Our increased flying habits are also taking a huge toll on the planet. Indeed, air traffic is the fastest growing source of CO_2 emissions. Not only does it produce large amounts of CO_2, however, it also destroys the countryside as airports expand. There is also the issue of increased road congestion and noise near airports. By 2030 it is thought that there will be 500 million plane passengers a year in the UK.[5] (For further information, see the Friends of the Earth website, www.foe.co.uk)

WHAT CAN I DO?

- *Instead of driving, can you walk or cycle shorter journeys (and lengthen your idea of what is 'short'!)?*
- *On fast roads, drive at 55 to 60 miles per hour instead of 70 (or more!). Anticipate what is ahead so that you accelerate and brake more gently, and try to move up the gears quickly.*
- *Can you holiday in the UK instead of abroad this year, or travel by train (see www.seat61.com)?*

◎ Engaging with God

Think about the worries and concerns you shared at the start of this session. Bring these issues to God (perhaps putting the pieces of paper in a bowl on a table), along with anything in the news this week that has especially shown the damage between God, people and the non-human creation. Ask for God's justice and righteousness to be known in these situations; thank Him for His mercy, His kindness and His love. Pray together for any troubled situations known to you in your own community.

GOD, THE PEOPLE AND THE LAND

◎ To open with

What is your favourite season of the year? Try to describe it using no more than seven evocative words.

◎ Read

Deuteronomy 28:1–24
Psalm 148
Jeremiah 5:20–29

◎ Thinking together

The Old Testament is a collection of books telling the story of God's workings for salvation through His chosen people, Israel. These books stretch over a time span of thousands of years. They represent many different settings, are written by very different people and in all manner of different styles. And yet, through this disparate mix of writings, the circle that we saw last week showing the relationship between God, people and the non-human creation is a continuous theme through it all.

The land is vital to the people of Israel. It is the locus of God's promises to them and a part of their identity, stretching right back to God's first call to Abram in Genesis 12:1. The land is given to Israel as the place in which they are to live faithfully for God, obeying His commands and living a life of righteousness and justice. The land is to be the place in and through which they fulfil God's words that the nation of Israel is to exist in order to be a blessing to 'all peoples on earth' (see Gen. 12:2–3). Note, with reference to Week Two, that 'earth' here is *adamah*. The land is never given to the Israelites in order for them to use it purely for themselves: God's blessings are to be shared.

Several important themes come out when we consider the place of the land in the life of Israel. The first is summed up in Psalm 24:1: 'The earth is the Lord's, and everything in it, the world, and all who live in it.' Whilst Canaan is 'the promised land', it is always recognised that ultimate ownership lies with Israel's God, Yahweh. The land is thus to be considered as a gift, and treated accordingly.

We see this in the way that the regulations regarding the Sabbath and Year of Jubilee are applied also to the land – and to animals, in the case of the Sabbath (see Lev. 25). The principles contained in such ancient institutions are remarkably relevant to us today. They speak of the importance of rest, both for humans and other species, and remind us of our need to rely not on our own abilities but on the faithfulness of God. They show us that because God has generously given the land, it should be used generously for the sake of others, not in order to increase one's own personal wealth. We also see this in, for example, the command against moving someone's boundary stone (Deut. 19:14). Thus the principles of justice and equality go hand in hand with acknowledging that the land is a gift from God.

Overall, the land acts as a sort of spiritual barometer, revealing the health or otherwise of the people's relationship with God. The connections are very clear: when the people follow Yahweh faithfully and worship only Him, this is seen by their practising social justice and care for the needy. The result of this is that all goes well in the land; there is fertility and climatic predictability. However, when the people turn away from Yahweh and follow other gods instead, then they forget to practise social justice and care for the needy. The result is that the land responds accordingly and revolts against them – there are upheavals in the land, and crops and animals fail. The Jeremiah section in the suggested readings this week is one of many passages that link these three together. (Amos 8 similarly is a very powerful passage.)

Finally, the Old Testament contains some wonderful passages that hint at the relationship that the non-human creation enjoys with the Lord, regardless of human beings. We hear that 'All the earth bows down to you; they sing praise to you, they sing praise to your name' (Psa. 66:4) and that 'The heavens declare the glory of God; the skies proclaim the work of his hands' (Psa. 19:1). It is humbling to see the evident delight that both God and His creation take in one another!

For discussion

- *We learn quite a lot about God, the land and the people from Leviticus 25. Read it through. Discuss what relevance you think this chapter has for us now?*
- *There is a great deal of emphasis on personal property and land rights today, but we read in Psalm 24 that 'The earth is the LORD's and everything in it' (v.1). How should this knowledge affect our attitude towards ownership and stewardship?*
- *Reflect on the earlier readings from Deuteronomy 28 and Jeremiah 5. Do you believe that the earth still acts as a spiritual barometer today? Why/ why not?*
- *'The heavens declare the glory of God; the skies proclaim the work of his hands' (Psa. 19:1). Read also Psalm 66:4. How do you think the non-human creation truly glorifies God?*

◎ The issue: Species extinction[6]

As I write this I can see the bees buzzing around my garden, collecting nectar on their constant rounds. The deep drone of a bumblebee is the very sound of summer. Yet, some are saying that by 2018 the British bee could be extinct. Albert Einstein famously said that if the bee were wiped out civilisation would end within eight years, and it is certainly true that, without the bee, we face very serious problems indeed.

The bee is but one species among many that faces extinction. The International Union for Conservation of Nature (IUCN) is the leading global expert on these issues. It produces the authoritative *Red List of Threatened Species* which classifies species according to their risk of global extinction. Their assessment in 2007 was that there are now 41,415 species on the IUCN *Red List* and 16,306 of them are threatened with extinction – in 2006, it was 16,118. One in four mammals, one in eight birds, one third of all amphibians and 70 per cent of the world's assessed plants on the 2007 IUCN *Red List* are in jeopardy (see www.iucnredlist.org for more information).

Some experts estimate that the rapid loss of species that we are witnessing today is between 100 and 1,000 times higher than the expected natural extinction rate (some studies estimate current extinction rates as 1,000– 11,000 times higher than natural rates). The current extinction phenomenon, unlike the mass-extinction events of geological history, is one for which a single species – humanity – seems to be almost wholly responsible. It is being referred to as 'the sixth extinction crisis', after the five known extinction waves in the Ordovician, Devonian, Permian, Triassic and Cretaceous Periods.

The reasons for this high rate of species extinction include the loss of habitat and its increasing fragmentation into smaller areas. The links with deforestation that we considered last week are obvious. Over-exploitation through hunting and fishing are other major causes, as is pollution. Then there is the invasion of 'alien' species which destroy native populations. Finally, looking back to Week One, climate change is having a significant impact on biodiversity and on the ability of species to survive.

◎ The response: The energy we use

I sometimes feel that it takes enough energy of my own to get from morning to evening in one piece without having to worry about any other sort of energy! But the reality is that my day uses up much more than just my physical and emotional energy. Have a think through your day. What have you done and what energy has that required? Maybe you have had a warm shower, boiled a kettle, made some toast, used the central heating, watched some television, drunk some water, listened to the radio, used cold milk from the fridge, used your computer … The list is endless. All these things require energy in some form or another, whether that be gas, electricity, petrol or diesel.

We might think that what we do every day is quite normal, but it is sobering to realise that, per capita, our CO_2 emissions are fifty times higher than they are in Bangladesh. In fact our energy uses are quite staggering and we have created a society that is completely dependent on using large amounts of energy, the majority of which is oil-based. In fact, globally nearly three-quarters of the energy we use comes from fossil fuels (in the UK that figure rises to nearly 90 per cent, and in the US to 85 per cent). The problem is that the energy comes at a price beyond that which we pay to our energy suppliers. The leading issue is climate change. However, there are other issues too, such as acid rain, which results in terrible damage to lakes and forests.

WHAT CAN I DO?

- *Try reducing the amount of energy you use. Shower instead of bath, turn down the central heating (and don't have it on as much), use low-energy light bulbs, turn all appliances off instead of using standby etc.*
- *Think about switching to a 'green' energy supplier. These need not necessarily be more expensive (Ecotricity, for example, will match the price of your local supplier; Good Energy is another good supplier).*
- *Send an email/letter to the Prime Minister asking the government to invest in renewable energy and take steps to radically reduce the country's CO_2 emissions (the Friends of the Earth website will provide helpful tips).*

◎ Engaging with God

Praise God that the earth is His, and everything in it. Thank Him for His amazing world, the sky, the land, the changing seasons, the diversity of people, animals, birds and insects. Remembering that He is Lord of all, ask Him to show you how you can more effectively live to please Him and bless others – humans, and the non-human creation! Reread, out loud, Psalm 148, as an act of worship. If appropriate, write a piece of prose, a poem or a song, giving glory to God for His creative work.

OUR FUTURE HOPE

◎ To open with

Try to imagine how the world will look in fifty or one hundred years' time. How would you *like* it to be, and why? Discuss.

◎ Read

Isaiah 65:17–25
Colossians 1:15–20
Romans 8:19–21
Revelation 4

◎ Thinking together

In this *Life Issues* study guide we have been considering what the Bible says to us in the face of the massive problems our world and its inhabitants face today. We have looked at the beginning: at how a loving God created a world that was 'very good' and was designed to have relationships at its heart. However, the Fall broke those relationships and resulted in intense disharmony on all levels. The rest of the Bible story tells of God's plans to put back to rights all this stuff that had gone wrong, starting with God's call to Abram in Genesis 12 and then continuing down through the Old Testament. As Christians we believe that God's plans find their fulfilment in Jesus; He came to bring to fulfilment all that Israel was called to be and do – to be a blessing to the nations and the means by which they were to be brought back into a worshipping relationship with God.

We often talk about the good news of Jesus in terms of salvation for people: God rescuing us from this earth in order to live out our final destiny in heaven. However, is that really what the Bible teaches? Let me make some brief points.

Firstly, salvation in Jesus Christ *is* offered to all people and, through that salvation, we gain eternal life. But – and this is crucial – this eternal life starts *now* and is not about going to heaven as our final resting place. Tom Wright, the Bishop of Durham and a leading biblical scholar, has made it clear that we rest in heaven until Jesus returns to this earth. Our final destiny is *this earth*, renewed and transformed and united with heaven.[7]

Secondly, are we wrong to think that salvation is only about people? The fact that this has been the predominant Christian view demonstrates how human-focused our thinking is. For example, the story of Noah is one that many of us have been brought up with as children, and yet have we noticed that the covenant God makes is not made with Noah alone, but with 'all living creatures/life on the earth' (a point that is emphasised six times in Genesis 9!)?

This exclusively human focus has likewise caused us to narrow our understanding of salvation. When we look at passages such as Romans 8:19–21 and Colossians 1:15–20 (and Ephesians 1:9–10) we see that God's plans for salvation, yes, are for people, but include *all* that He has made. Colossians 1:19 states this explicitly and makes the remarkable assertion that Jesus' blood was shed on the cross 'to reconcile to himself all things'.

Finally, what about where it says that this earth will be destroyed? This understanding is taken primarily from 2 Peter 3 (especially vv.10–11). However, whilst the AV translated verse 10 as saying that 'the earth … and the works that are therein shall be burned up', more recent translations (eg the NIV) based on earlier manuscripts now say that 'the earth … will be laid bare'. The Greek word is that from which we get our word 'eureka!' and has positive overtones of being discovered. In other words, when Jesus returns to this earth and the fire of judgment comes, what is evil will be burned up so that what is good will be seen (like gold in the refiner's fire). In the same way that the judgment in Noah's day did not absolutely destroy the world (see v.6), neither will the final judgment. Thus, the Greek word for 'new' in Isaiah 65:17 (reflected in Revelation 21:1 and 5) is less about destroying something in order to make a new thing, and more about renewal and transformation.

◎ For discussion

- *Have these thoughts about how 'the environment' fits into God's plans for salvation challenged your own ideas? How, and why?*
- *Read Matthew 6:9–13. What do you think it means for God's will to be done on earth as it is in heaven?*
- *Think through your own beliefs about the ultimate future. How have these influenced the way you view/care for the world?*
- *What is the most important thing you have learned from this study about what the Bible says about humanity's relationships with the earth, each other, and God?*

◎ The issue: Water

A friend of mine volunteered in a Tanzanian leprosy village. When I asked what difference it had made to her, she said that she now could not turn on a tap without thinking of the situation she had left behind. For those of us in economically developed countries, water is something we hardly think about. We use it constantly throughout the day without giving it a second thought. Whilst we may sometimes have the inconvenience of floods and droughts, we are far removed from what so many others are experiencing around our world. Today, 41 per cent of the world's population (that's 2.3 billion people) are living in areas with water problems, where water is either not easily available and/or is of poor quality. It is thought that by 2025, two in every three people will live in such areas of 'water stress' and that by 2050 nearly half of the world's population will face severe shortages.

The reason for this is the global demand for water, which is currently increasing at more than double the rate of population growth. We might think we do not use much water: maybe we have showers instead of baths and we drink a bit of water during the day, but actually our water usage is hidden behind our other activities (this is called 'virtual water'). So, for example, it is shocking to realise that a burger takes 2,400 litres of water to produce, a (non-organic) cotton T-shirt takes 2,700 litres and a pint of milk 1,760 litres (for more on this see www.waterfootprint.org). Whilst we should not restrict our discussion of water usage to food alone (industrial products are very water intensive), it is interesting to note that a vegetarian diet requires around 2.6m^3 of water a day, whilst a USA-style meat-based diet requires over 5m^3.

In the UK, whilst the situation might not appear as horrendous as it is elsewhere, still over-extraction is leading to falling water tables and this is affecting the ecosystems that depend on them. So, for example, an English Nature survey found that one in ten freshwater wetland Sites of Special Scientific Interest (SSSIs) in England is threatened by water extraction. Globally, in the last three decades of the previous century, numbers of freshwater birds, fish, mammals and amphibians halved.

The response: The things we throw away

Did you know that we never throw anything away, we just throw it somewhere else? And that 'somewhere else' is primarily landfill tips. Despite our increasing interest in recycling, the majority of stuff that we do not want any more still ends up at the dump. In the UK, a whopping 90 per cent of rubbish is buried in landfill sites (in the USA that figure is 55 per cent). In general, recycling rates are improving massively, with UK households now recycling 32 per cent, but non-household waste lags far behind and pulls down the national average.

The problem with landfill sites is that the biodegrading rubbish produces CO_2 and methane, which both of course contribute to climate change. It also produces toxins which leach into the ground and then into underground water sources. Every time we throw something away and replace it with a new product we are using up raw materials. Not only does this put intense pressure on the earth, but those raw materials are often extracted in ways that are detrimental to the local people and their immediate land.

WHAT CAN I DO?

- *Reduce! We are constantly being encouraged to consume – buy more clothes, a nicer car, the latest electrical equipment and so on. But the Bible tells us to be content with what we have, and to keep ourselves free from the love of money (see Heb. 13:5).*
- *Re-use! Take things to a charity shop; sign up to Freecycle (www.freecycle.org); hold 'swap-shop' parties with friends; use washable nappies; turn vegetable containers into trays for sowing seeds; re-use plastic bags; turn plastic bottles into bird feeders; try to mend rather than replace, etc.*
- *Recycle! Install a water butt; never throw away anything if it can be recycled; talk to your local council about increasing their recycling facilities; take all packaging back to the supermarket each week and ask the manager to recycle it!; look at www.recyclethis.co.uk for lots of tips and ideas.*

Engaging with God

In the light of all that you have learned in the past four weeks, spend time asking God what He is saying about the way you live your life in relation to the environment. Ask Him to show you how you can please Him as you honour His creation. Is there anything He would like you to do today, this week, this month? Make notes and share together what you believe God is saying to you. Finish by thanking Jesus for His glorious future, a future He has planned for good.

Notes

[1] R. Middleton and B. Walsh, *Truth is Stranger than it Used to Be: Biblical Faith in a Postmodern Age* (London: SPCK, 1995), p.123.

[2] My thanks go to the Old Testament scholar Chris Wright for this. For more on ecology in the Old Testament see Chapter 4, 'Ecology and the Earth', in his *Old Testament Ethics for the People of God* (Leicester: IVP, 2004). Chris is careful to emphasise that this grammatical reading does not mean that humans are made *only* to look after God's world. Interestingly, the most recent NIV version has changed its translation of this verse to read this way.

[3] From the IPCC WG1 Summary for Policy Makers 2007 report: http://www.ipcc.ch/ipccreports/ar4-wg1.htm

[4] Report 'Livestock's Long Shadow' (2006) from FAO's website, www.fao.org

[5] Projection made by John Spellar MP, then Transport Minister, 2002. (Original source unknown.)

[6] Much of the information in this section comes from the IUCN (www.iucn.org).

[7] It is hard in such a short space to do justice to a concept which, for many, will be a new way of looking at some key Christian beliefs. I would recommend Tom Wright's *New Heavens, New Earth: The Biblical Picture of Christian Hope* (Cambridge: Grove Books, 2006, second edition). It is an inexpensive, accessible and helpful introduction to this subject.

FURTHER READING

- D. Bookless, *Planetwise* (Leicester: IVP, 2008). An in-depth but easy to read exploration of the biblical material with practical ideas too.
- R. Valerio, *L is for Lifestyle: Christian Living that Doesn't Cost the Earth* (Leicester: IVP, 2008). A practical, biblical A–Z of caring for our world and its inhabitants, both human and non-human.

RESOURCES

- A Rocha. An international and UK-based Christian environmental charity helping care for creation and transform communities, especially through practical, local conservation projects (www.arocha.org.uk).
- Christian Ecology Link. A multi-denominational UK Christian organisation for people concerned about the environment (www.christian-ecology.org.uk).
- www.livinglightly24-1.org.uk – a website dedicated to helping us live simpler, greener lives.

OTHER RESOURCES FROM CWR...

Other titles in the *Life Issues* series

Forgiveness, Ron Kallmier
ISBN: 978-1-85345-446-2

Relationships, Lynn Penson
ISBN: 978-1-85345-447-9

Work, Beverley Shepherd
ISBN: 978-1-85345-480-6

We currently have seven daily dated Bible reading notes. These aim to encourage people of all ages to meet with God regularly in His Word and to apply that Word to their everyday lives and relationships.

Every Day with Jesus - devotional readings for adults. ISSN: 0967-1889
Inspiring Women Every Day - for women. ISSN: 1478-050X
Lucas on Life Every Day - life-application notes. ISSN: 1744-0122
Cover to Cover Every Day - deeper biblical understanding. ISSN: 1744-0114
Mettle - for 14-18s. ISSN: 1747-1974
YP's - for 11-15s. ISSN: 1365-5841
Topz - for 7-11s. ISSN: 0967-1307

£2.49 each per bimonthly issue (except *Mettle*: £4.49 per four-month issue) from January 2009.

Get the benefit of Insight

The *Waverley Abbey Insight Series* gives practical and biblical explorations of common problems, valuable both for sufferers and for carers. These books, sourced from material first presented at Insight Days by CWR at Waverley Abbey House, offer clear insight, teaching and help on a growing range of subjects and issues.

Self-esteem: 978-1-85345-409-7
Eating Disorders: 978-1-85345-410-3
Stress: 978-1-85345-384-7

Bereavement: 978-1-85345-385-4
Anxiety: 978-1-85345-436-3
Anger: 978-1-85345-437-0

£7.50 each

Courses from CWR

We run a range of biblically-based training courses at our headquarters of Waverley Abbey House, Farnham, Surrey, England. These include courses on counselling and on life issues such as forgiveness.

For more details, call our Training Department on **+44 (0)1252 784700** or visit our website: **www.cwr.org.uk**

Prices correct at time of going to print.

National Distributors

UK: (and countries not listed below)
CWR, Waverley Abbey House, Waverley Lane, Farnham, Surrey GU9 8EP.
Tel: (01252) 784700 Outside UK (44) 1252 784700

AUSTRALIA: CMC Australasia, PO Box 519, Belmont, Victoria 3216.
Tel: (03) 5241 3288 Fax: (03) 5241 3290

CANADA: David C Cook Distribution Canada, PO Box 98, 55 Woodslee Avenue, Paris, Ontario N3L 3E5. Tel: 1800 263 2664

GHANA: Challenge Enterprises of Ghana, PO Box 5723, Accra.
Tel: (021) 222437/223249 Fax: (021) 226227

HONG KONG: Cross Communications Ltd, 1/F, 562A Nathan Road, Kowloon.
Tel: 2780 1188 Fax: 2770 6229

INDIA: Crystal Communications, 10-3-18/4/1, East Marredpalli, Secunderabad – 500026, Andhra Pradesh. Tel/Fax: (040) 27737145

KENYA: Keswick Books and Gifts Ltd, PO Box 10242, Nairobi.
Tel: (02) 331692/226047 Fax: (02) 728557

MALAYSIA: Salvation Book Centre (M) Sdn Bhd, 23 Jalan SS 2/64, 47300 Petaling Jaya, Selangor. Tel: (03) 78766411/78766797 Fax: (03) 78757066/78756360

NEW ZEALAND: CMC Australasia, PO Box 303298, North Harbour, Auckland 0751.
Tel: 0800 449 408 Fax: 0800 449 049

NIGERIA: FBFM, Helen Baugh House, 96 St Finbarr's College Road, Akoka, Lagos.
Tel: (01) 7747429/4700218/825775/827264

PHILIPPINES: OMF Literature Inc, 776 Boni Avenue, Mandaluyong City.
Tel: (02) 531 2183 Fax: (02) 531 1960

SINGAPORE: Alby Commercial Enterprises Pte Ltd, 95 Kallang Avenue #04-00, AIS Industrial Building, 339420. Tel: (65) 629 27238 Fax: (65) 629 27235

SOUTH AFRICA: Struik Christian Books, 80 MacKenzie Street, PO Box 1144, Cape Town 8000. Tel: (021) 462 4360 Fax: (021) 461 3612

SRI LANKA: Christombu Publications (Pvt) Ltd, Bartleet House, 65 Braybrooke Place, Colombo 2. Tel: (9411) 2421073/2447665

TANZANIA: CLC Christian Book Centre, PO Box 1384, Mkwepu Street, Dar es Salaam.
Tel/Fax: (022) 2119439

USA: David C Cook Distribution Canada, PO Box 98, 55 Woodslee Avenue, Paris, Ontario N3L 3E5, Canada. Tel: 1800 263 2664

ZIMBABWE: Word of Life Books (Pvt) Ltd, Christian Media Centre, 8 Aberdeen Road, Avondale, PO Box A480 Avondale, Harare. Tel: (04) 333355 or 091301188

For email addresses, visit the CWR website: www.cwr.org.uk

CWR is a Registered Charity – Number 294387

CWR is a Limited Company registered in England – Registration Number 1990308